YOU CAN TEACH YOURSELF®
TO COMPOSE MUSIC

D1606806

4/2005

CD CONTENTS

1	Rec. #1 [0:26]	20	Rec. #20 [0:14]	39	Rec. #39 [0:21]
2	Rec. #2 [0:43]	21	Rec. #21 [0:40]	40	Rec. #40 [1:53]
3	Rec. #3 [0:12]	22	Rec. #22 [0:39]	41	Rec. #41 [1:12]
4	Rec. #4 [0:14]	23	Rec. #23 [1:32]	42	Rec. #42 [1:15]
5	Rec. #5 [0:25]	24	Rec. #24 [1:30]	43	Rec. #43 [1:17]
6	Rec. #6 [0:45]	25	Rec. #25 [0:26]	44	Rec. #44 [1:22]
7	Rec. #7 [0:25]	26	Rec. #26 [0:39]	45	Rec. #45 [0:13]
8	Rec. #8 [0:15]	27	Rec. #27 [1:40]	46	Rec. #46 [0:12]
9	Rec. #9 [0:22]	28	Rec. #28 [0:44]	47	Rec. #47 [0:13]
10	Rec. #10 [0:20]	29	Rec. #29 [0:48]	48	Rec. #48 [0:12]
11	Rec. #11 [0:46]	30	Rec. #30 [1:14]	49	Rec. #49 [0:13]
12	Rec. #12 [0:46]	31	Rec. #31 [0:34]	50	Rec. #50 [0:13]
13	Rec. #13 [0:24]	32	Rec. #32 [0:35]	51	Rec. #51 [0:25]
14	Rec. #14 [0:15]	33	Rec. #33 [1:24]	52	Rec. #52 [0:21]
15	Rec. #15 [0:13]	34	Rec. #34 [0:15]	53	Rec. #53 [0:53]
16	Rec. #16 [0:12]	35	Rec. #35 [0:34]	54	Rec. #54 [1:02]
17	Rec. #17 [0:14]	36	Rec. #36 [0:15]	55	Rec. #55 [0:23]
18	Rec. #18 [0:24]	37	Rec. #37 [0:17]	56	Rec. #56 [0:31]
19	Rec. #19 [0:31]	38	Rec. #38 [0:15]	57	Rec. #57 [0:30]

3 3988 1004 3920 4

MEL BAY

© 1996 BY MEL BAY PUBLICATIONS, INC., PACIFIC, MO 63069.
ALL RIGHTS RESERVED. INTERNATIONAL COPYRIGHT SECURED. B.M.I. MADE AND PRINTED IN U.S.A.

Visit us on the Web at http://www.melbay.com — E-mail us at email@melbay.com

3

CONTENTS

PREFACE 5
ABOUT THE AUTHORS 6

Part I

WHERE DO I START? 7
THE BASICS YOU SHOULD KNOW TO WRITE A SONG 7
  A song's component parts; Notation; Kinds of notes; Time signatures
DIVIDING YOUR SONG INTO MEASURES 8
IDEA PEOPLE, SONGWRITERS, AND COMPOSERS 8
DEVELOPING YOUR INNER EAR 9
INTERVALS 10
DEFINING THE SCALE 11
"HEARING" A MELODY IN YOUR HEAD 11

Part II

IS THERE ONLY ONE METHOD BY WHICH WE CAN COMPOSE? 13
COMPOSING BY SIGHT 13
STEPS, SKIPS, AND LEAPS IN MELODY WRITING 14
WHAT GOES UP MUST COME DOWN 15
A GOOD PATTERN IS WORTH REPEATING 16
SEQUENCE: IT'S MUCH LIKE A PATTERN BUT HAS A SLIGHTLY DIFFERENT TWIST 17
WHAT BEGINS MUST END 17
THE NEED FOR A CADENCE WITHIN A SONG 18

Part III

RHYTHM: WHERE COMPOSING MUSIC REALLY COUNTS 21
  Determining the pulse of the song; The transfer from pulse to note
AT LEAST ONE MILLION MELODIES WAITING TO BE DISCOVERED 24
  Telephone book number method

Part IV

WRITING THE LYRICS TO A SONG 27
  Re-writing the lyrics to an old standard; Finding the syllable pattern; Making the lyric make sense
ARE WE CERTAIN WE UNDERSTAND RHYME? 28
WHAT ABOUT USING FREE VERSE IN LYRICS? 29
ONE OTHER THING: ACCENTED BEAT 29

Part V

PREFACE

This book is an answer to a question we have been asked frequently: Can you help me write a song? There seems to be a strong desire in many individuals to share creatively the feelings they hold inside. It is our hope that this book will help open doors and lead the way to the completion of your individual project.

It is with this in mind that we have included a variety of approaches to composing. Some are intended to start you on the most difficult task: notating music on staff paper. Until you learn, practice, and perfect this process, you will always be dependent on someone to take your "musical dictation," and you will fall short of completing the total process. Take time to learn to notate music—by sight, by lyrics, by using models—until you have a firm grasp of the skills needed to accomplish this process.

Next, begin to notate what you hear in your mind, first putting down the notes on the staff, then figuring out the rhythm, then dividing it all into measures. Add the time and key signatures, trying different chords until you have selected the proper chord progressions for your masterpiece. A step further would lead you to orchestrate your song for instruments or arrange it for voices.

Here are some suggestions to help you better understand the text:

1. FIND a musical resource person to whom you can turn if you get "stuck." Although the book contains all the information you need, you may need help occasionally putting all the pieces together. There are people all across the country who understand the musical language and can be of help. The kid next door who plays drums far into the night is probably well acquainted with rhythm patterns. Churches, schools, and private piano studios contain people whose lives consist of helping people understand music. Use them!

2. BE PATIENT. If you are a beginner, work the simpler sections of the text thoroughly until they are in-grained. Start with simple melodies and rhythms and gradually progress to more difficult ones.

3. DO the exercises rather than just read them. The instructions will be more understandable if you are in-volved in the exercise.

4. USE this text at your own level. If you are presently ready to orchestrate, then skip to that section.

5. PRODUCE your song and bring it to completion, Yes, it does require perseverance, but the reward is great. Whey you allow someone else to perform your song and you hear it for the first time, we're certain you'll be motivated to try it again! GOOD LUCK!

ABOUT THE AUTHORS

You can rest assured everything you find in this book will work effectively! Bob Ashton and Nancy Colbaugh (co-authors) have practiced their own methods for many years, resulting in hundreds of published and/or recorded works.

Both are ASCAP composers. Both are educators having taught K–12 and college-level students for more than a combined sixty years! Their seminars are among the most highly respected involving creative work.

Individuals of national prominence have used their expertise to further their creative output. Who knows! *You* may be next!

PART I

Where Do I Start?

That's a logical question. Its answer depends on where you now are. Few people begin at the same spot. Determining your musical locale will help you to plot your course more effectively. (Take the quiz in Appendix A. Allow 15 minutes or less.)

But the important question is, Can you compose a song? Are you gifted enough in this particular area? Although the following statement is, as yet, only theoretical, we believe it has much validity: The extent of your ability to perform any task is directly related to the intensity of your desire to perform this task. Unless you are willing to "move mountains" in order to write music, you probably won't leave posterity much of a treasure. Yet, you might leave some very lovely knickknacks if you wish to pursue composing in a more limited manner.

What are the skills you must have, and which of these skills do you now possess? Music is a language and, like other languages, must be mastered before it can be put to use. Lines, spaces, note symbols, time signatures, rhythm patterns, harmonic structures, and a host of nuances team up to speak a language universally received by ear. But to write the language you must know it!

The following pages give a smattering of the basics needed to make the most elementary design we call music. Become well acquainted with these pages as a first step in writing a song.

The Basics You Should Know to Write a Song

Music (song) has three parts (and in music to be sung, a fourth part).

  a. MELODY: the going up and down of various pitches or tones as indicated by notes.
  b. RHYTHM: how long each note is held.
  c. HARMONY: the combination of various notes sounded/played simultaneously or within a sequence of time that is influenced by the other NOTES.
  d. LYRICS: the words to a song.

NOTATION is placing the melody on staff paper alone or with other notes necessary for the completion of the song as an arrangement.

  a. A staff has five lines and four spaces.

    Any extra lines needed to place notes either higher or lower than the lines on the staff are called *ledger lines*.

  b. There are two staffs in common use:

    TREBLE CLEF 𝄞 The names of the lines are E-G-B-D-F; spaces are F-A-C-E.

    BASS CLEF 𝄢 The names of the lines are G-B-D-F-A; the spaces are A-C-E-G.

  c. Music uses only the alphabetical letters ranging from A to G. Once you get to G, you start over with the letter A and continue to go to G. This process may be continued for as long as you have space to write.

    KINDS OF NOTES (necessary to produce the rhythm desired when used in conjunction with a certain time signature):

| Whole note | o | Half note | ♩ | Quarter note | ♩ |
| Eighth note | ♪ | Sixteenth note | ♬ | | |

Triplets   (three notes played in the time of two of the SAME KIND)

Remember: The only way the above notes have a SPECIFIC time value is to use them in accordance with a TIME SIGNATURE.

TIME SIGNATURE: Tells how many beats (or counts) there are to a measure and then tells WHAT KIND OF NOTE gets ONE count.

    a. The TOP number tells how many counts there are to the measure:

$$\frac{4\ (4)}{4} \qquad \frac{6\ (6)}{8} \qquad \frac{2\ (2)}{4} \qquad \frac{3\ (3)}{4} \qquad \frac{12\ (12)}{8}$$

    b. The BOTTOM number tells what kind of note gets ONE count. The number 2 stands for a half note, 4 stands for a quarter note, 8 stands for an eighth note, and 16 stands for a sixteenth note. Example: In 4/4 time, there are FOUR beats to a measure, and a QUARTER note gets ONE count (see Appendix D).

Dividing Your Song into Measures

A measure is an arbitrary division of a song into a unit of pulse, or beat, determined by the time signature placed at the beginning of the song (or at some new place in the song, when a change is being made). The vertical lines separating the measures are called measure bars or bar lines.

As a minimum, your song must have a staff, a clef sign, a key signature, a time signature, notes to complete each measure, chord symbols, and words (if it is to be sung).

Example:

Oh,   give   me   a   home,   where   the   buf – fa – lo

Idea People, Songwriters, and Composers

Idea people are those who have a suggestion for a song (either the lyric or the melody) and have neither initiated a beginning nor conceived an ending. The counterpart to this individual is the one who approaches the storywriter and says, "Why don't you write a story about . . . ," but lacks the skills necessary to communicate his or her idea effectively. Patience and perseverance seldom find a home in this person's creative nest.

Songwriters are those who can conceive a melody (and lyric if it entails one) and who can reasonable play, sing, or write the melody on the staff so that it can be played or arranged by another. Essentially, the creator of this new song has constructed it from start to finish and has relatively solid ideas about its key, rhythm, and chord structure.

There really aren't very many composers. A composer has concrete ideas about all of the above and carries his or her musical construct to its completion. In addition to supplying introductions, endings, and so on, the composer writes the accompaniment, chooses and places the chord symbols to coincide with the harmonic structure used, and ensures that the musical interpretation is integrated throughout the course of the song. And, more often than not, the composer classifies his or her song in the stricter classical form and arranges it appropriately for formal use, strictly adhering to the capabilities of the intended performers.

Because our goal is to develop composers, we will address all of you in the future-potential mode and use the term *composer* throughout the text.

Developing Your Inner Ear

A common complaint we hear from potential composers is that the song is locked inside with no way to be exposed. If we could simply "look" into the mind, we could "see" the ideas for a song, or we could hear what the songwriter is hearing. This gap can be bridged, but it will take some effort.

A musical language must be learned. Its uniqueness might be compared to sign language for a deaf person. Its purpose is to enable the inner song to be notated. There is a great feeling of joy and accomplishment as you hear your song being played and sung by someone who is simply reading the notation you have given him or her. Every phase and nuance of your song can be notated so that the singer/player can perform it the way you desire.

We will present some simple procedures that will enable you to progress to the place where you CAN bring that song from your head and heart to staff paper.

A Good Song Versus a Bad Song

What is a good song? What is a bad song? That's not easily answered. The purist will no doubt tie your song's construction to that of a traditional image. Yet, taste—that is, personal taste—is really the dominant factor in determining what is good and/or bad in any art form.

The greatest motivation one can latch on to is this: Be content with nothing but your finest effort. When *you* are pleased with your song—so much so that you *must* share it with others—you're well on your way to becoming a composer of worth.

Use this chart to develop inner hearing by singing easy intervals, such as 1–5 and 1–3. Add more difficult intervals after easier ones have been mastered.

Sing through any simple song substituting interval numbers for words.

Create harmony by having two groups of students sing different scale numbers at the same time. A leader or teacher can direct by pointing to two different sets of vertical numbers. Singers will hold the note until a new number is indicated. Keep it simple!

As a class, begin to sing a well-known song. On a given clue, "sing" silently until a second clue is given to resume audible sound. This may be repeated throughout the remainder of the song, demonstrating the students' ability to hear intervals.

Do 8 (1)

Ti 7

La 6

Sol 5

Fa 4

Mi 3

Re 2

Do 1

Intervals

The musical scale is to your song what words are to your story. The more you understand the "language" and how it relates, the more complex a song you can create.

What is an interval? An interval is the distance between one note and the next in reference to pitch. Using numbers, we can simply count one note to the next to find the interval (or the distance between them in pitch).

Example:

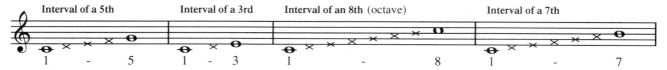

Because we are in the key of C, C becomes number 1 and counting from C to G in the alphabet we have a spread of five, or a 5th. The x's represent the steps between the two notes.

Use the numbers 1, 2, 3, 4, and 5 to write a song. Put them in any order, but start and end on 1. Put four numbers in each measure.

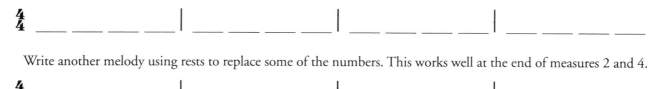

Write another melody using rests to replace some of the numbers. This works well at the end of measures 2 and 4.

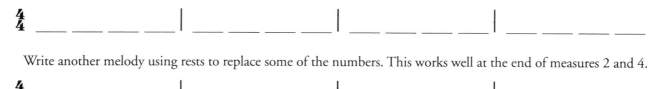

Assign numbers to notes on the staff in the key of C: C = 1, D = 2, E = 3, F = 4, and G = 5. (The same is applicable to any other key. Example: In the key of F, F = 1, G = 2, A = 3, B♭ = 4, C = 5, D = 6, E = 7, and F = 8).

Write a melody on the staff using the numbers from one of the songs above and place the notes correctly on the staff.

Example:

Defining the Scale

There are three practical ways to define any scale. As an example, let's use the C scale:

C	D	E	F	G	A	B	C
1	2	3	4	5	6	7	8
Do	Re	Mi	Fa	Sol	La	Ti	Do

Because it was the C scale, you will note that it begins with the *root*, or *tonic*, note C and proceeds on to the C one octave (eight notes) above it. Now we could have used the second method and begun with the number 1 and proceeded to the number 8. Or, the use of the syllables "Do Re Mi" and so on would have accomplished the same thing.

SCALE NAMES: This was the first method above. An instrumentalist first learns the names of the notes and the corresponding way to create that note on any given instrument. The note C will be C no matter what part of the world it is played in. This is called a *fixed scale*.

NUMBERS: The second method involves the numbers 1 through 8. The number 1 can be assigned to the first note of any scale (in this case, the note C), and each sequential note receives the next number until the number 8 is reached. Because low C and high C in a scale are the same name, the number 1 can replace the 8 at the end of the scale.

SOL-FEG: In a pattern similar to the numeral system, the word (or syllable) "Do" is shown to denote the first note of the scale. And, of course, we go up the scale, with each tone being given a different syllable. This method is widely used by singers. It is named the "movable Do" because the syllable "Do" can be used to show the first note of any scale, whether it be C, G, F, or whatever.

If you can understand the fixed scale and how it progresses, then you are ready to begin singing it without the aid of an instrument. YOU HAVE STARTED TO DEVELOP YOUR INNER EAR!

Take it a step further and begin to sing C–G–C (or 1–5–1, or Do–So–Do) interval after interval until they become so ingrained in your memory they become a simple operation requiring minimal effort to perform. This should include all possible combinations.

"Hearing" a Melody in Your Mind

This is an absolute must on your list of needs in becoming a composer. Let's pursue the following steps for a trial run:

a. Can you silently hear *The Star Spangled Banner* without audibly sounding your voice? Does it help to form the words.

b. Silently sing the simple eight-tone major scale using the syllables "Do Re Mi" and so on. Now take your hand and begin waist high with "Do." Raise your hand a few inches with each successive pitch until you have gone one octave up to "Do." Now begin on the upper "Do" and come back down using the same hand "language."

c. Can you do the half steps of the scale? Starting at the bottom and progressing up the scale by half steps, use your hand language in this manner. There are thirteen steps in this chromatic scale:

$$\frac{13}{C}$$

$$\frac{12}{B}$$

$$\frac{11}{A\#/B\flat}$$

$$\frac{10}{A}$$

$$\frac{9}{G\#/A\flat}$$

$$\frac{8}{G}$$

$$\frac{7}{F\#/G\flat}$$

$$\frac{6}{F}$$

$$\frac{5}{E}$$

$$\frac{4}{D\#/E\flat}$$

$$\frac{3}{D}$$

$$\frac{2}{C\#/D\flat}$$

$$\frac{1}{C}$$

d. Let's take the song *America*. Place the words above, even with, or below each other according to the melody you hear in your mind. Let us help you get started:

Now let's draw some lines to indicate the length of time each note is held. For those notes held the same length of time, use the same length of line. Notes held for a little longer get longer lines, and shorter-held notes get shorter lines. Same song! *America.* We'll start it for you, then you finish it:

___   ___   ___   _____   __   ___

PART II

Is There Only One Method by Which We Can Compose?

Not at all. Several methods will produce compositions that will meet certain requirements. However, simply as a starting point, let's pursue composing by sight.

Composing by Sight

It is possible to compose a song using only the "sight sense." In fact, it is a good place to start for beginning composers because many lessons can be learned that pertain to future development.

Most people balk at this method because they cannot hear what they are writing, making it seem like a mental exercise as opposed to an exercise in creativity. The following is an excellent exercise.

Start with the basic elements of music:

1. On staff paper, draw a treble clef sign. This will be at the beginning of each new line of music.

2. Determine what key your song will be in. At this point, choose only the key of C, G, or F. If necessary, turn to Appendix B for key signatures to be copied. The following example is the key of G. (In Example 1, there is neither a sharp nor a flat. This indicates that the song is in the key of C, which requires no sharps or flats.)

3. Choose a time signature for your song. This choice is limited (for now) to $\frac{4}{4}$ or $\frac{3}{4}$ time. Our example will use $\frac{4}{4}$ time.

4. Because our example is in the key of G, we will choose our first note from the G chord (see Appendix C for notes of various chords). You can now see that our choice is either G, B, or D as these three notes make us the root (or tonic) chord for that key (root or tonic chord, meaning the first three notes of any chord). Note: You do not HAVE to select one of the root notes for your beginning. It simply is the safest way to go at first.

5. Because we have chosen the key of G, let's be certain to end our song on the note G. Virtually all songs end on the note of the tonic, root, or key-signature name.

We are now ready to start our song. A few simple rules, however, must be followed to ensure success.

Steps, Skips, and Leaps in Melody Writing

Most popular songs (songs having great public appeal) follow the pattern of many steps, some skips, and only a few (if any) leaps. Music written not following this formula is usually difficult to perform and often difficult to remember. In other words, as a beginning effort, let's keep it simple. Of course, there are songs that successfully use leaps. A good example is the song *Over the Rainbow,* but it IS an exception!

For our purpose, and while we are exploring the beginnings of this creative process, we are going to set some boundaries for ourselves. When first composing, use STEPS only, then progress to STEPS and SKIPS, then add LEAPS (if you find them necessary) until you are able to determine on your own which will sound best. Remember, you are entering a whole new world—a new language—and these boundaries will help you feel somewhat safe in these new surroundings. Listen now to recording 1 playing steps, skips, and leaps. (These are played on an oboe for clarity of pitch.)

How They Are Made

(Recording No. 1)

A step is a note moving from line to space or from space to line.

A skip is a note moving from line to line or from space to space.

A leap is a note moving a greater distance than either a step or a skip.

The "La-La" Song

(Recording No. 2)

Examples of steps, skips and leaps:

BANC

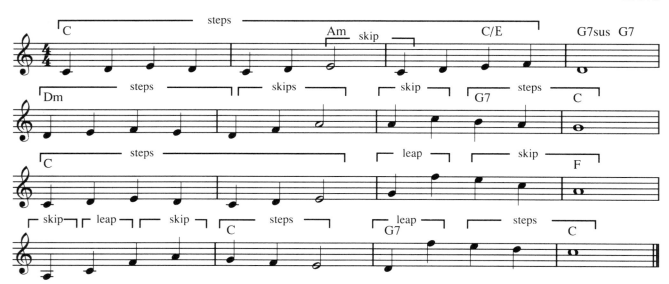

Let's pratice writing some steps, skips, and leaps.

Put four quarter notes in each measure using steps. Play on keyboard or bells.

Put four quarter notes in each measure using skips. Play on keyboard or bells.

Put four quarter notes in each measure using leaps. Play on keyboard or bells.

Put four quarter notes in each measure using steps, skips, and leaps.

What Goes Up Must Come Down

(Recording No. 3)

It is a simple admonition, but one that is well taken by the young composer. If the notes are ascending, then let them return by steps, skips, or leaps. Although our desired outcome is not that each melody look like a perfect wave pattern (), it is wise to stay within the staff when beginning and to check to see how your melody looks.

Now, back to our song. Using what we have learned, let's begin to compose one measure of notation:

We have completed four beats, which is the number of beats we have chosen for each measure. Now we draw a bar line to indicate the end of our measure. Now, let's finish our song, making it a four-measure melody. Use a double bar at the end to indicate that the song is finished, at least at that point.

(Recording No. 4)

Did you notice that we ended the song on the note G? Because we said that this would be a four-measure melody, it signified that the entire song would consist of only four measures. That, at least in the beginning stages of composing, required us to end on G, which is the name of the key in which we were writing our song. Had this been only a portion of a song in the key of G, we could have ended on another note, with the idea in mind that we would ultimately end on the note G.

A Good Pattern Is Worth Repeating

Let's just suppose that the previous four-measure melody was simply the first four measures of a longer song. Could we use that same pattern for the next four measures? Yes, very effectively! In fact, this is very often done by changing the second four measures only slightly. Notice how we used the first two measures exactly as they are and changed (only slightly) the last two:

(Recording No. 5)

Well, that was easy! And it sounds quite musical, doesn't it? It can still be continued, but with a slight change. And there is good reason for doing so. A major key to song popularity is its simplicity and relative ease by which it can be quickly learned. Okay, with a nice chord change at the end of the twelfth measure, we can virtually repeat measure 1 through 8 and finish the song as though it were a sixteen-measure melody. Let's see how it works (we've added an organ to the oboe melody to let you hear how chords change a song to fit your liking):

(Recording No. 6)

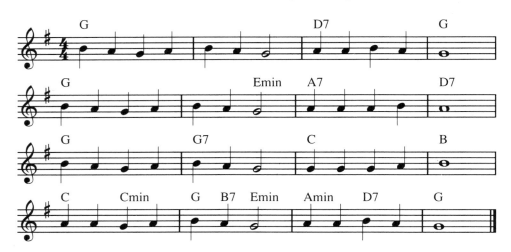

Too much change makes a song too hard to learn; at least a song like the above (designed for the less sophisticated ear) would have been too complicated without the repeated patterns.

Compose a four-measure pattern using steps and skips and one or two leaps. Play on keyboard or bells.

When you are satisfied with the pattern, copy it below and repeat it, adding an ending.

Try again, writing a new pattern.

Sequence: It's Much Like a Pattern but Has a Slightly Different Twist

Pattern suggests, "If it works once, why not try it again?"

This is the underlying principle of pattern. It also applies to sequence. Patterns and sequence make songs popular or, at least, are part of the process.

Let's do one more pattern just to get it more thoroughly in mind. Here it is demonstrated in *Mary Had a Little Lamb:*

(Recording No. 7)

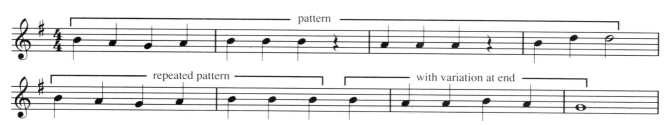

Sequence differs from a pattern in that it starts on a different note but follows the same melodic pattern, either exactly or with a slight variation. *Three Blind Mice* offers a good example of sequence.

(Recording No. 8)

Of course, a more complex song will contain a more complex sequence, but the principle is the same. Songs without pattern and/or sequence find popularity an uphill climb. Keep this in mind: As a beginning composer, you will follow the conventional route. Later, you will incorporate the new and unusual. Any well-trained athlete begins with the warm-up period and saves his or her best effort for the time of challenge. Good musicianship demands the same conditioning. The exploration of the unknown can be accomplished only after the known has been carefully studied and used.

What Begins Must End

A time signature demands that each measure contain an appropriate number of counts. The key signature gives each measure considerably more freedom. But we do have some guidelines that keep us in line (musically speaking) so that we tend to have a home base. We have called it the root (or tonic) chord, tonality, or key. Now, there is a term coming into current usage called *home tone.* It is the same as *root* or *tonic.*

We use the term *home tone* as being synonymous with *tonic, root,* or *tone center* because it quite effectively tells what is happening in the music or, at least, what should happen. Look at the following example. You supply the last tone. If you don't get this one right, you may well have a problem following conventional patterns. Here it is:

(Recording No. 9)

Here's another example: Try playing or singing *Twinkle, Twinkle, Little Star* but do not play or sing the final note. Normally, you should experience a feeling of frustration as the song come to its final root, tonic, tonal center, or home tone, only to find that you have stopped short of finishing the song by one note. Why? Because music normally wants to end on the same note as the key signature by which it is named, that is, the root, tonic, tonal center, or home tone. Have we made our point?

The Need for a Cadence within a Song

A particular problem of young composers is the lack of cadences occurring within the body of their song. This leaves a feeling of wandering, purposelessness, or never-ending fragments that come to no completion. When this occurs, it signifies a lack of cadence.

A cadence is simply a resting place so that the melody does not go on endlessly. For example, in the song *Home on the Range* you find the initial musical phrase saying, "Oh, give me a home, where the buffalo roam, where the deer and the antelope play." That ends in a cadence. Now, when it continues, it more or less does a repetition of the first part, with a bit of change at the end, and then comes to a second cadence.

Then, too, the cadence often gives the singer (or instrumentalist) an opportunity to take a breath. Listeners, likewise, enjoy the opportunity to take a mental break!

(Recording No. 10)

In any given key, the interval of a second, or a fifth, offers an excellent opportunity to invent a cadence melodically. The example to follow uses the interval of a second:

Cadence is also necessary in the rhythm of a song. Although it will be dealt with more completely in a later section, let us say now that at the point where the cadence is felt (melodically), a note with a longer value is usually in good taste.

Nearly all songs end on a home tone, that is, the note of the key in which the song is written. For example, the home tone for the key of F is the note F, and that for the key of G is the note G.

Let's listen to two songs—one without a cadence and one with a cadence. The one without a cadence will bore you to tears!

The "No Cadence Song"
(Recording No. 11)

BANC

The "Cadence Song"
(Recording No. 12)

BANC

A cadence is simply a resting place so that the melody does not go on endlessly. Normal conversation needs a cadence, or resting place. Provide the cadence for these sentences:

He ran down the _____.

She straightened out her _____.

They started to _____.

We finally _____.

Notice that:

1. there is more than one correct answer,

2. the sentence is incomplete without the last word(s), and

3. the words before the end need to lead sensibly to the last word.

In music, the need for your song to "make sense" depends on how you use the cadence.

How many ways can you reach the home tone? Let's try a few to see. Complete the next three two-measure melodies. (Notice the key signatures!)

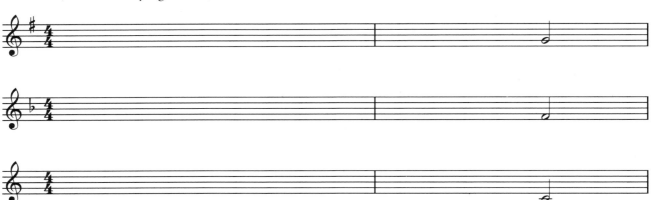

PART III

Rhythm: Where Composing Music Really Counts

Here's where your time signature dictates the flow of your composition. It's the heartbeat of the song, the very pulse that makes your creative work healthy. Skip a beat and you've thrown everything into a quandary.

But it needn't be so challenging that it becomes a roadblock. Take it easy, and make it simple. As you progress into musical maturity, the rhythm problems no longer pose such threats as they do at first.

A common problem is the premature use of intricate rhythms, resulting in unsingable (or nonplayable) melodies. Although students often enjoy drawing eighth and sixteenth notes on the staff, they need to be reminded to reserve those notes for other times, not when beginning to compose.

The use (or incorporation) of lyrics often helps in determining the pulse of a song. First, find the pulse in the lyric before you attempt anything else. Then try to determine where the accent (or strong beat) occurs. Think in terms of either three or four counts per measure as these are the most common meters (or time signatures) in music. Call the accented beat "one" and the following beat "and." The following example helps to depict this method:

(Recording No. 13)

>		>		>		>	
1	&	2	&	3	&	4	&
Run -	ning	wa -	ter	com -	ing	quick -	ly

>		>		>		>	
1	&	2	&	3	&	4	&
Cov -	ers	all	the	dry	brown	earth	

>		>		>		>	
1	&	2	&	3	&	4	&
Gig -	gling,	bub -	bling,	laugh -	ing,	chuck -	ling,

>		>		>		>	
1	&	2	&	3	&	4	&
Tell	me	where	you	find	such	mirth?	

Now suppose you were to keep the same pulse (or beat) as that above but say your words twice as fast. You will find the need for sixteenth notes:

(Recording No. 14)

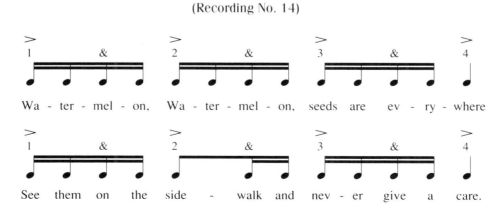

Wa - ter - mel - on, Wa - ter - mel - on, seeds are ev - ry - where

See them on the side - walk and nev - er give a care.

It is obvious that no one can sing or play your song correctly unless it is notated accurately, both melodically and rhythmically. Another approach is to use a grid, which is showing the shortest beat in the song. Let's go back to *Twinkle, Twinkle, Little Star* for a try at this particular process.

For this song, we're going to use dots in place of notes. (Actually, you can use x's, circles, or whatever, but the important thing is that something is being put down on paper to indicate rhythm.) The first step is to find the shortest beat in the song. You do this by singing (or playing) the song. When you find two or more notes that move more quickly than the others, begin tapping at the speed of those notes.

As we sing, "Twink-le, twink-le, lit-tle, star . . . ," we find that "star" is the only long beat in that phrase. All the other syllables are the same. So here is how it looks with dots:

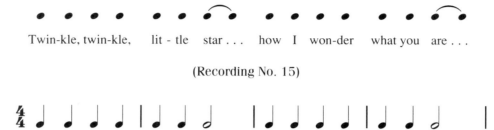

(Recording No. 15)

See how simple it is to transfer the dots into notes and place the measure bars where they belong!

Now let's go to one just a bit more difficult: *Home on the Range.* As we sing for a few measures, we find that the words "where the" are the shortest, so we use them as the speed for each dot.

(Recording No. 16)

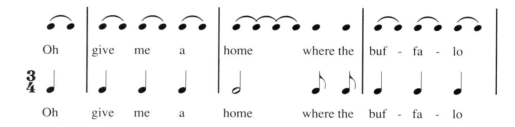

Use this page to figure out the rhythm of a song. Each dot represents the shortest sound in the song. Finish the example by placing the words under the dots, tying dots together for longer sounds, as in the first two lines.

> Baa, baa, black sheep,
> Have you any wool?
> Yes sir, yes sir,
> Three bags full.
> One for the master,
> One for the dame,
> One for the little boy who lives in the lane.

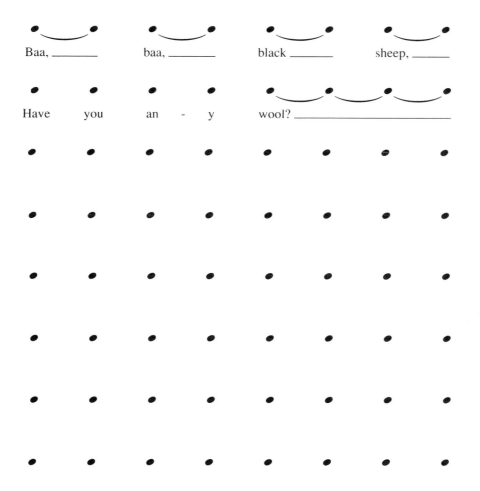

Finish these rhythm patterns.

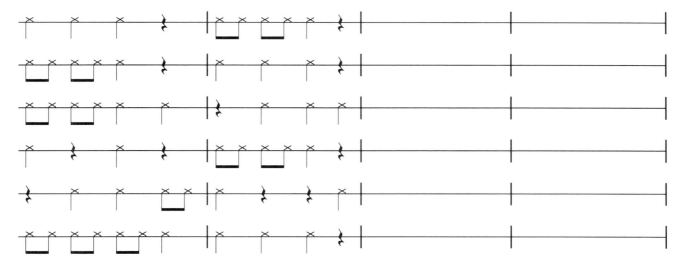

Write a short rhythmic pattern, two or four measures long, with a repeat sign. Play rhythms simultaneously on various unpitched instruments. Add piano improvisation or use a recording with the same meter.

Baseball ostinato (do this with your friends): Have small groups choose a baseball chant, such as "Hit the ball" or "Keep your eye on the ball." These chants should be done in rhythm.

Example:

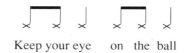

Keep your eye   on the ball

Starting with one chant, add additional chants until the entire group is participating. You can use various dynamic levels and accents, finishing by stopping each group one by one until only one group is left chanting. Add some interest by having each person chant (in rhythm) his or her favorite ball team and end with everyone chanting the local team(s) and "Play ball!"

At Least One Million Melodies Waiting to Be Discovered

It's true! There is a source of melodic inspiration available in every household. It's the telephone book! Because the musical scale ranges from 1 to 8, you can assign numbers to each note in the scale, such as C-1, D-2, E-3, F-4, G-5, A-6, B-7, and C-8. (C-8 means that the C is an octave above the first one used, C-1.)

Now you simply pick out any number in your telephone directory and assign each number a note on the scale. The number 881-5463 (in the key of C) would be CCCGFAE. Several numbers might be worked together to form a song, too. Suppose we were to take the latter approach and add the numbers 265-4352. (This can be a group activity if you wish.) Watch for a cadence!

Here's how it appears using both sets of numbers:

(Recording No. 17)

Now, should you want to use this musical phrase as a short song, simply go back to the beginning (the first three measures) and change the last (or fourth) measure, resolving the cadence. (Remember "pattern and sequence.") Placing chords above the notes will add another dimension of sound:

(Recording No. 18)

Notice how the last measure resolves the melody to a state of rest. Singing (or playing) it with the proper cadence makes a SONG out of it rather than a mere collection of notes. Also note that we ended in C—the name of our key.

Just for the fun of it, let's add some words to our song. Or, as the more proper musical term, let's add the lyrics to the telephone number song. Here's ours—you can add your own. (Wait for the two-measure introduction before you start to sing with the recording.):

(Recording No. 19)

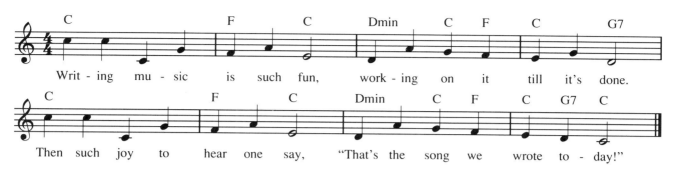

Writ - ing mu - sic is such fun, work - ing on it till it's done.

Then such joy to hear one say, "That's the song we wrote to - day!"

Write a song using a telephone number: ___ ___ ___ – ___ ___ ___ ___
(my telephone number)

1. Take your seven-digit phone number and assign a musical letter for each number.

C = 1   D = 2   E = 3   F = 4   G = 5   A = 6   B = 7   C = 8

omit #9 or assign it D, one octave higher than 2
omit #0 or assign it B, one note lower than 1

2. Place notes on the staff in the order of your phone number (here 651-2355):
   Example:

6   5   1   2   3   5   5

3. Divide measures into four counts each.

4. You may lengthen the telephone song by adding pattern and sequence or by using another telephone number.

5. Make necessary changes at cadence points so that your song makes sense. Write lyrics to your melody.

PART IV

Writing the Lyrics to a Song

The lyric is the straight-forward message of your song. Other more subtle messages are given out through the melody, rhythm, and harmony involved. The lyric must say something that correlates with the subtle message of the music itself. For example, the music to the hymn *The Old Rugged Cross* hardly makes a sound bed for a nonsensical rock-and-roll composition. In other words, one segment must compliment the other.

Just for a start, let's take an old standard song, *Home on the Range,* and rewrite the lyric. First, as it is.

(5) <u>Oh, give me a <u>home</u></u>

(6) <u>Where the buffalo <u>roam</u></u>

(9) <u>Where the deer and the antelope <u>play</u></u> . . .

(5) <u>Where seldom is <u>heard</u></u>

(6) <u>A discouraging <u>word</u></u>

(9) <u>And the skies are not cloudy all <u>day</u></u> . . .

Notice that we have counted each syllable and found the pattern to be 5, 6, 9 . . . 5, 6, 9. That is, five syllables in the first line, six syllables in the next, and then nine syllables with the three dots following. (The three dots indicate a pause, or cadence). Then comes the identical pattern repeated: 5, 6, 9 . . . 5, 6, 9, and a stanza (or verse) has been created.

To rewrite the above lyric (using the same melody), let's create a syllable pattern first and then begin to fill in our lyrical thoughts:

(5) ___ ___ ___ ___ ___

(6) ___ ___ ___ ___ ___ ___

(9) ___ ___ ___ ___ ___ ___ ___ ___ ___

(5) ___ ___ ___ ___ ___

(6) ___ ___ ___ ___ ___ ___

(9) ___ ___ ___ ___ ___ ___ ___ ___ ___

Notice that we have double-underlined those words that rhyme and triple-underlined those words that rhyme, that is, home-roam, heard-word, play-day. Ready? Let's do one! First, draw your syllable lines in the 5, 6, 9 . . . 5, 6, 9 pattern:

(5) <u>I'd like to go <u>back</u></u>

(6) <u>To a place on the <u>rack</u></u>

(9) <u>With a hole in the bottom so <u>blue</u></u> . . .

(5) <u>Perhaps I might <u>train</u></u>

(6) <u>Some old dog by its <u>mane</u></u>

(9) <u>And be known as the one who knew <u>you</u></u> . . .

Heavens! What's wrong? Well, it just doesn't make sense! It is not enough simply to follow pattern with words that rhyme. A lyric (a GOOD lyric) MUST make sense and cause someone to reflect favorably on what has been said. The more persistent the reflection, the better the lyric.

Okay, let's rewrite the above lyric and do a better job. Here goes!

(5) <u>I'd like to go <u>back</u></u>

(6) <u>To that tumbl'd down <u>shack</u></u>

(9) <u>By the lake with its water so <u>blue</u></u> . . .

(5) <u>Perhaps there could <u>be</u></u>

(6) <u>Someone there just for me</u>

(9) <u>Oh, I wish that sweet some one were you</u> . . .

Ah! That's better. Oh yes, one further thought. Must the rhyme ALWAYS occur at the END of the line? Hardly. It may occur ANYWHERE, as long as it serves the purpose.

Example:

> I saw a little kitten
> Sittin' by the house . . .
> Chances are, its glances are
> About to see a mouse . . .

Here we find "kitten-sittin'" in rhyme and the phrases "chances are" and "glances are" in semi-rhyme (we say "semi" because the words "are" and "are" are identical, not rhyming, words), and "house" and "mouse" are found in the more conventional position for rhyme. All of it works.

Are We Certain We Understand Rhyme?

Do your rhyming words actually rhyme? Or are they merely close? For example, do these words really rhyme?

> stars . . . ours
> cars . . . wars

Well, if you are playing horseshoes, you will probably get points for being close, but in songwriting it's usually not the case. Let's rhyme the above words correctly:

> stars . . . cars
> ours . . . flowers
> wars . . . pours

Which brings us to another point about rhyming verse. Why does rhyming verse often appear to be trite? Mainly because it does not make lyrical sense, nor does it contribute to the proper emotional release often seeming contrived simply for its own sake. The following original poem should tend to prove our point. The setting: A man and woman who were once deeply in love have a serious disagreement, resulting in his permanent departure from her life. She stands looking out the window as he leaves. Tears flow down her cheeks:

> TEARS
> It couldn't change a thing, she knew
> The door had clos'd behind . . .
> For only one sheds tears for two
> When someone's been unkind . . .
> But what is left? Can words convey
> The emptiness within?
> No, tears are marks upon the heart
> To show where love has been . . .

The rhyme hasn't been contrived. The words used seem to be very appropriate to the message. It's simply not trite.

What about Using Free Verse in Lyrics

Good Idea! But are you sure you know what *free verse* really is? Is it really free? That is, is it really formless and, in a sense, fancy-free? Hardly. Perhaps the most misleading statement concerning free verse is found in the faulty teaching of "type-set" poetry, whereby it is taught as being poetry in the form of free verse.

The following is an example of typeset free verse, which is neither free verse nor poetry. It is only typeset!

> A summer's day
> Has started hot and dry.
> The sky is
> Oh, so blue!
> Somewhere, overhead
> A bird sings

Here is the above "poem" as it really is—prose!

> A summer's day has started hot and dry. The sky is
> oh, so blue! Somewhere overhead, a bird sings.

Free verse (as either a lyric or a poem) MUST have some justification (preferably by form) in order to qualify as free verse. The following original lyric is contained in the song *Autumn Farewell*, published by Hinshaw Publishing Company under the collective title *Serenity*.

> AUTUMN FAREWELL
> Autumn whispers its last goodbye
> With winds of gentle behavior . . .
> Nature's palette of Autumn hues
> Soon will yield naught but grey . . .
> Too soon will winter put birds to flight;
> Too soon will night wear her crown . . .
> Autumn whispers its last goodbye
> And beckons the leaves to lie down . . .

The two verses opening with "too soon" establish a form. The ending rhyme of "crown and down" establish another. Its syllable meter is 8, 8, 8, 6, 9, 7, 8, 8. Through comparatively vague, form DOES exist.

One Other Thing: Accented Beat

You can fill in the syllable blanks, make it rhyme, and still have little to offer if your accented beat is misplaced. May we use our old favorite one more time?

Here's an example of misplaced accent had the songwriter chosen to write it like this:

> Give mé a home whére
> The buffálo roam thére . . .

We don't have to go further—it just doesn't work! The accented beat falls on the words "me," "where," "fa," and "there." In the original version, it would look like this:

> Oh, gíve me a hóme
> Where the búffalo róam

The accented beats on "give," "home," "buf," and "roam" work out because we say búf-fa-lo, not buf-fá-lo (see Appendix F for another example).

The Lyric as a Tool for Note Placement

You can gain much help in note placement by saying your lyric out loud and placing a measure bar ahead of the strong beat, which NORMALLY opens each new measure. Of course, more sophisticated writing breaks this rule; but for now, let's start with the concept of a strong beat opening each measure.

Home on the Range is written in $\frac{3}{4}$ time. We have already concluded that "give" is the first strong beat, so we must assume "Oh" to start ahead of the measure bar, or it becomes (in musical terms) a pickup note.

Example:

> Oh, | gíve me a | hóme where the | búffalo |
> | róam, where the | déer and the | ántelope |
> | pláy...... | ......where |

Now, as we analyze the above, we must begin to interpret sounds into rhythm patterns. We know that in $\frac{3}{4}$ time there are three beats to a measure and that a quarter note gets one count. As you look at the word "Oh," you realize it is the last count of a preceding measure or a count of an opening song. So let's give it a quarter note value like this and draw a measure bar to begin the song:

Oh,

Now, speak aloud the next three words "give me a." Do they sound equal in length of time as you say them? Right! And there are three of them in a row, so what do we do to get three counts in that measure? You are right, again! We use three quarter notes:

Oh,   give   me   a

Next, we come to the need for getting a beat established. I know you have often been taught not to tap your foot to the beat, but let's fudge just for a time or two, okay? Start by tapping the strong beat "one" with the heel of your left foot and tapping "two-three" with the heel of your right foot. Okay, let's review the above: Begin tapping, left, right, right, left, right, right, and so on, until you feel a groove for the beat of the song. Now, on the second "right" say the word "Oh" as the pickup tone and go on with the next measure saying "give me a." Do this several times until it begins to feel natural.

Fine! Let's go on. Here is something new! The word "home" begins on the left foot and takes one beat with the right foot also. How come? Because it is a half note! Now, another new one! When your right foot hits the floor again and starts to come up for another beat, you have already said two words: "where the." What do we do with the two words on one beat? We use eighth notes (because it takes two eighth notes to equal one quarter note). Here is how it looks:

Oh,   give   me   a   home   where the

Ready to go on to "buffalo"? Okay, say it aloud, and you will find another three equal pulses (beats), one for each syllable. Well, we need only three beats for each measure, so it looks like this:

Oh,   give   me   a   home   where the   buf - fa - lo

Now, lets assume you can figure out the next few syllables until we come to a totally new situation. The word "play" seems to go on for five counts., How do we handle this? We use what is called a *tie,* that is, an arc-drawn line that ties one note over to another for more counts than the one note can give. One more new concept we have to introduce is the *dotted note.* A dot behind a note increases its value by one half. Because a half note gets two counts in $\frac{3}{4}$ time, then a dot will add one half of two (or one more count), making a dotted half note worth three counts. That's all we need for one measure, so we dot the first half note and then tie it over to the next measure's half ($\downarrow$) note (two counts) for the full five counts needed. Here's our song as we now have it:

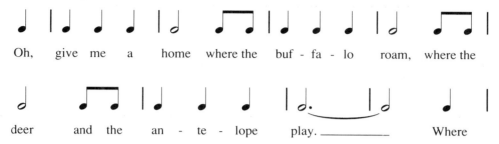

Well, that's the hard part. The easy part is to go to the keyboard (or do it in your mind) and find the correct-sounding notes to place on the staff, and you have graduated into a songwriter who can make up his own lead sheet.

Composing by Lyric

(Recording No. 20)

Now we will actually write an original song using a prescribed lyric. You, the composer, will set your own melody to the words. There are several ways to approach this method. You might want to write the melody by "ear," by "harmonic structure," or by the "sight" of a melodic line. Use one note per word or syllable, with each pulse or beat being indicated by an underline.

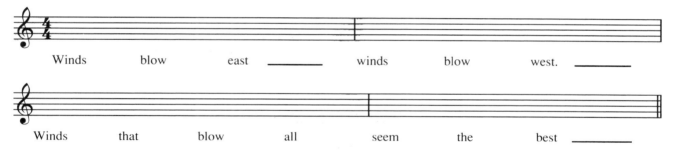

Now, let's try putting quarter notes and quarter rests on the staff and see how the song will sound. This is an example only—you make up your own.

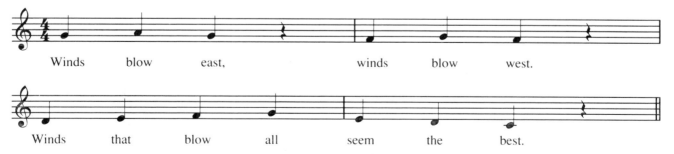

Make up your own lyric, similar to *Winds Blow East*. Divide the lyrics into measures. Add notation.

Did you rhyme your lyric? You don't have to. One last little tip about finding rhyming words: Take the syllable or word you are trying to rhyme and, beginning with "a," proceed throughout the alphabet. Suppose the word were "fat." Begin with aat, bat, cat, dat, eat, gat, hat, iat, jat, kat, lat, mat, nat, oat, pat, qat, rat, sat, tat, uat, vat, wat, xat, yat, zat, and so on.

Enlarging the Scope of Lyric Writing

(Recording No. 21)

How might we enlarge on this concept and contribute toward a more enterprising effort? Among other ways, one can take a well-recognized public domain song, supply new lyrics, and include it in a musical. The following example is from an Ashton-Colbaugh music-drama concerning human rights:

The time:	Mid-1860s
Setting:	Lincoln, seated behind his desk, stage right. (Actor wears Lincoln mask; lights are semi-bright on stage.) Across from Lincoln, stage left, a small chorus of multi-ethnic costumed singers begin to sing Part II of the public domain standard, *Battle Hymn of the Republic* (see below for Part I and Part II lyrics.) (A cheesecloth screen separates singers from Lincoln and the audience, giving a veiled effect.)
Singers:	Sing Part II (Key of G).
Lincoln:	(Rises halfway through the above song, stands, shades his eyes, look at singers, and speaks.) I see you now! (Accompaniment softly changes to key of A-flat as Lincoln is speaking.)
Lincoln and singers:	Lincoln sings Part I as singers continue to softly sing Part II under his vocal solo. Volume of Part II depends on volume of Part I.

Lyrics to Part I:

Key of A-flat
Our eyes shall see the coming
Of respect for ev'ry man . . .
There shall be a banner lifted high
That says, "Today, we can!"
Ev'ry human shall declare his right
To live a life that's free . . .
At last, our liberty!

Key of A-natural
The shackles of the past have been
Removed from ev'ry limb . . .
We are free to be united, free to
Claim each precious hymn . . .
Ev'ry race, or creed, or color now can
Live a life that's free . . .
As last, our liberty!

Lyrics to Part II:

Glory, glory, hallelujah,
Glory, glory, hallelujah,
Glory, glory, hallelujah,
At last, our liberty!

Composing by Use of a Countermelody or Partner Song

What is a countermelody? Basically, it's a melody that is different from, but sounds well with, another melody. Usually, it carries the same message, almost as though is were part of the same song. And, usually, this is true. However, it is not bound to such a rule. A partner-song differs from a countermelody in that it usually is a song entity in its own right and uniquely fits into the picture being played or is sung simultaneously with the original melody.

In both cases, the same chord structure is used and, more than likely, the same time and key signatures. Exceptions do occur, but they are rare.

Why are they used? Well, they provide unique ways of having two or more songs harmonize. It is often easier to teach a second song as opposed to a second part. In other words, it becomes a musical entity in its own right and can be learned and performed as such. For people who must sing the melody, it gives both performers a melody to sing.

How are they written? There are no set rules for writing either a countermelody or a partner song, but there ARE some guidelines that tend to make the song more interesting. Among these are the following:

1. Use contrary motion where plausible.
2. Use different note values and rhythmic patterns when matching measure for measure.
3. Use the added harmonies beyond the tonic (or triad stage) of a chord. For instance, in a B-flat chord, we have the notes B-flat, D, and F. If we add the 6th of the chord, we have the additional note G. Passing notes may be acceptable, too.
4. Where possible (and in good taste), use words that rhyme or are identical when you come to a cadence.

For an example or two, the following countermelody from *Twinkle, Twinkle, Little Star* will provide you with a melody that follows the original lyric rather closely. Even if you heard it by itself, you would probably make connection with the fact that it was a part of the original song. Sing along and see how it works:

Twinkle, Twinkle, Little Star

(Recording No. 22)

arr. Ashton/Colbaugh

Composing by Following a Set Pattern of Chords and Note Values

Yes, you may place the notes wherever you wish. However, remember to apply all the principles of writing a song you have learned so far.

Each measure has a chord symbol indicating that you may use *only* those notes found in that particular chord! (Use Appendix C if you need help.)

At the bottom of the song, you will find all the chords used in the song and the notes that make up these chords. Also, you will find examples of all notes and/or rests required in the directions.

But first, let's listen to a recording of a song (using this same format) written by some of the students (grades 3 through 8) at the School of the Osage located in Lake Ozark, Missouri. They are part of the Gifted Program directed by Barbara Duffy. You'll hear their melody played on the cello. The lyrics are printed in line 1:

(Recording No. 23)

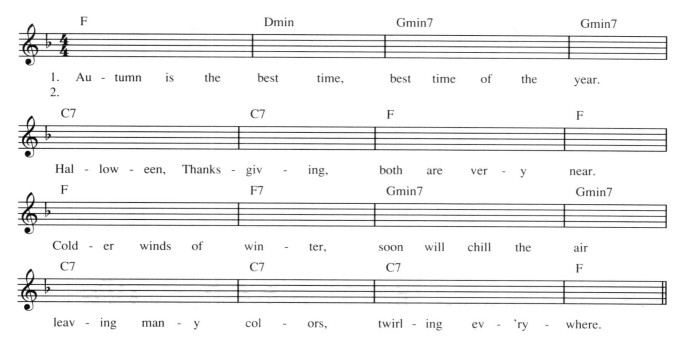

Are you ready to write your own? Let's try! The same accompaniment you heard on the last song will also work for your song. Write *your* melody and play *your* lyrics in the second lyric line.

(Recording No. 24)

Directions:

Measure
1: Use 4 quarter notes.
2: Use 2 half notes.
3: Use 4 quarter notes.
4: Use 1 whole note.
5: Use 4 quarter notes.
6: Use 2 half notes.
7: Use 4 quarter notes (4th note may be a passing note).
8: Use a dotted half note followed by a quarter-note rest.
9: Use 4 quarter notes. The 4th note may be a passing note.
10: Use 2 half notes.
11: Use 4 quarter notes.
12: Use 1 whole note.
13: Use 4 quarter notes. The 4th note may be a passing note.
14: Use 2 half notes.
15: Use 4 quarter notes (3rd note may be passing).
16: Use a dotted half note with a quarter-note rest.

Below are the chords you'll be using and the kinds of notes and rests you'll need:

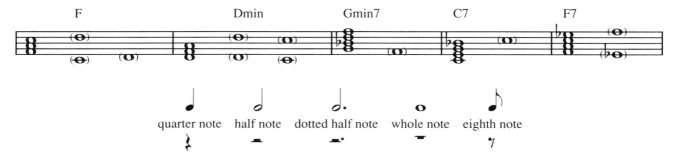

Directions for writing the lyrics (words) to your song about Autumn:

1. Your first line must have six syllables. your second line must have five. The third must have six, and the fourth must have five. The same pattern will apply to the second stanza (or group of four lines).

2. The doubled lines (2 and 4) must rhyme. (same for 6 and 8)

3. Your lyrics should tell a story. It should make good sense, and if well done it will stir the emotions of both the writer and the reader or listener. Everything about your words should relate to your title about the season, Autumn.

4. Copy your lyrics under the proper syllables of your song. Now sing it!

(Song Title)

_____

_____

_____

_____

_____

_____

_____

Now that you have the idea well established, let's try one more. Remember: Contrary motion works very well, and note values of different types than used in the melody offer favorable variety. (Have a friend play the original melody while you play your new countermelody—it should sound great!)

Write a contermelody using the chords of the original melody as your guide.

(Recording No. 25)

The following songs are well known to millions of music lovers. Both have orchestrations to enhance the sound of the original melody and your countermelody.

As you listen to the accompaniment, you will hear many countermelodies already in use. No, they have not *all* been taken. There are many, many more waiting for you to write them down.

Good luck!

Shenandoah and Counter Melody

(Recording No. 26)

arr. BANC

Write a contermelody to fit this song. (When listening to the recording, wait for the six-measure introduction to be played before the traditional melody begins.)

Aura Lee

Traditional

arr. BANC

(Recording No. 27)

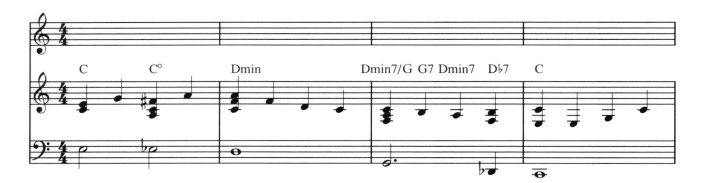

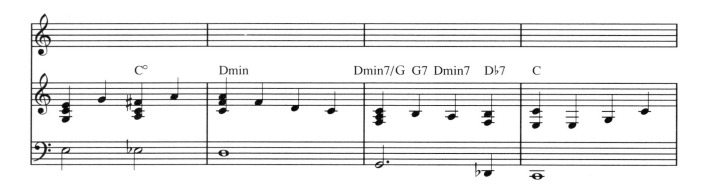

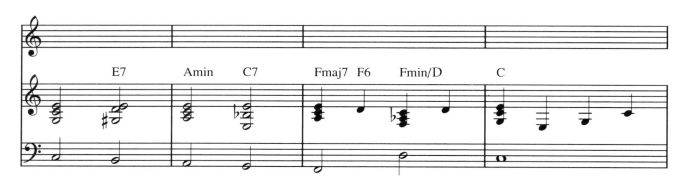

For a listening example of a partner song, we have included the song *Two Christmas Partner Songs*. The last two pages of this selection have been used by permission of Cambiata Press. These two songs are quite different in both melodic and lyric content, but they come together in use, depicting the season of the year associated with Christmas.

Two Christmas Partner Songs

(SC with Piano)

(Recording No. 28)

Words and Music by
Bob B. Ashton, ASCAP

One of the most entertaining pursuits of music arrangers involves the simultaneous use of two or more easily recognized songs, which provides both varied rhythmic and lyrical differences while remaining harmonically constant. Below is a relatively good example of using four partner songs at one time (wait for the intro!):

Partner Songs with Traditional Tunes

(Recording No. 29)

BANC

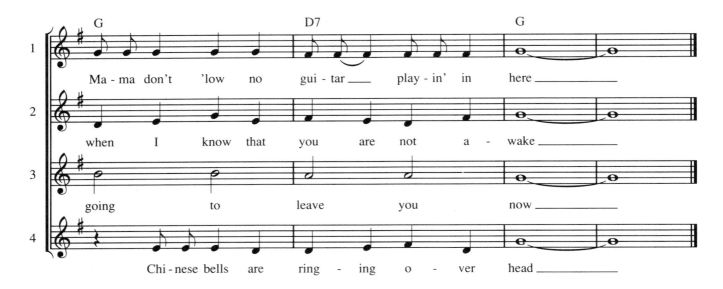

Composing with a Theme in Mind

More often than not, a composer has a visual (as well as audio) picture in mind in which some image is portrayed through music. Many facets of one's imagination go into play to form an overall effect that causes the listener-performer to make this creative connection with the composer.

In the following excerpt from the song *Night Lights,* both the melody and the lyrics add subtle nuances to the message of God's love and protection.

It is *arranged* for two equal voices. This has reference to types of voices and not to equal emphasis of parts as in a partner song. The melody is clearly found in the bottom part and is of more significance than the "harmony" part written above.

Let's listen to a portion of this song. The accompaniment has been orchestrated (used by permission of Hinshaw Music, Inc.).

Nightlights

for Two Equal Voices, with Piano

(Recording No. 30)

Words and Music by
NANCY COLBAUGH
arr. by Bob B. Ashton

Piano

The stars are clear this moon-lit night; ___
A world with man - y hid - den things; ___

bright - ly, on a clear and moon-lit night; ___ Like ___
beau - ty, with so man - y hid - den things; ___ He re -

Oh, the stars shine ver - y
made a world fill'd with

blink their mes - sage clear. _____ "When you
fright - en'd deep in - side. _____ Just look

blink their mes - sage clear. _____ "When you
fright - en'd deep in - side. _____ Just look

look up in the dark - ness, we are
up and see the twink - 'ling of the

look up in the dark - ness, we are
up and see the twink - 'ling of the

here in the sky.")
stars in the sky.)

here in the sky.")
stars in the sky.)

You

The Blues: The Loosest Form of Lyric and Melody

If boundaries are your hangup, try the blues. The blues always works, and if it doesn't, you then have something to write about!

It is certainly not new. And, as loose as it is, it's one of the most structured of all musical forms. It is twelve measures long, usually the same basic progression of chords, and lyrically of the negative connotation.

In other words, do it wrong and it's not the blues. "The St. Louis Blues" is certainly not the blues, *Kansas City* is!

Throughout the world, musicians can meet and instantly begin to improvise around the blues progressions because of its structure. No other musical form can make this claim.

Here is the twelve-measure form using the key of C. Some sample lyrics are given. Now, try your own. (For the most part, in place of the tonic chord, you can add the 7th according to your taste. Also, four beats, eight beats, or "boogie" beats are acceptable and normal.) Chords for line 1 are pure basic, and chords for line 2 are acceptable changes.

The Blues
(Recording Nos. 31 & 32)

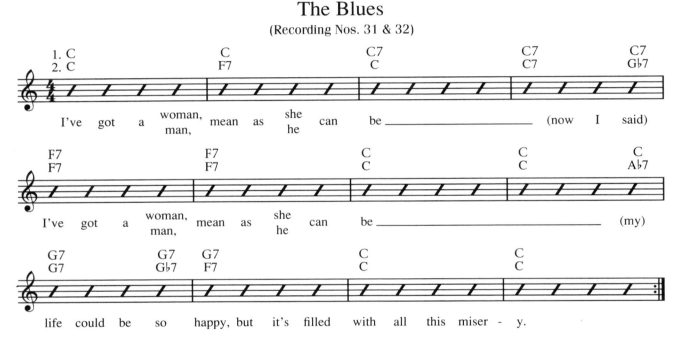

As you listen to the two recordings, you'll find that the first follows the chords in line 1 and that the second follows the chords in line 2. Sing along and make up your own lyrics!

Composing a Fugue

Johann Sebastian Bach is often said to be the most brilliant composer of the musical structure called the *fugue*. Even so, he did not always write his fugues according to the definite form suggested by today's musical scholars. To approach composing this musical structure called the fugue, we will take the simplest course possible.

These keys will be used in the fugue (follow fugue model, page 00):

Step 1: Write a short eight-measure melody following the chord symbols given in the fugue model. The notes in each measure should be the same as the notes in the chord, with the addition of some passing tones. The melody should begin on the 5th of its beginning chord.

Example: A of the D-minor chord, which contains these notes:

D	F	A
1	3	5

(Refer to Appendix B for a more complete explanation of how to name chords.)

Your melody should end on the root note of the ending chord, which is the *same chord* as at the beginning.

Example: D of the D-minor chord

Step 2: Write the same melody you wrote in step one, a 4th higher in the key of G-minor. In this key, your first note should be D and your last note G.

Example:

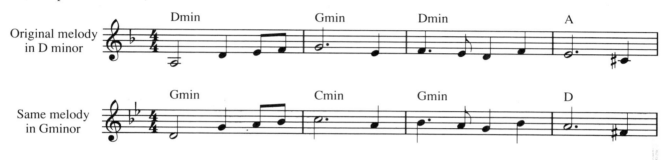

(This process is called *transposing*.)

Step 3:

Begin a new melody in the key of G-minor, using the same chord structure as transposed from the key of D-minor. Try to use different rhythms from that used in the previous melody.

Example:

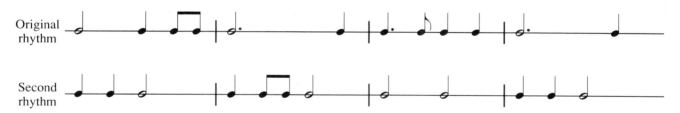

Rhythm patterns that work favorable are always worth repeating.

Step 4: Transpose melodies 1 and 2 into the new key of C-minor.

Step 5: Begin a new melody in the key of C-minor, using the same chord structure as transposed from the key of G-minor.

Step 6: Transpose melodies 1, 2, and 3 into the new key of F-minor.

Step 7: Begin a new melody in the key of F-minor, using the same chord structure as transposed from the key of C-minor.

Play your fugue, adding each new melody. If you have followed the chord structure in each key, and if the rhythms compliment each other, the results should be pleasing!

Now let's listen to an original fugue following the seven steps suggested. If your original melody tends to get too high on the staff, do as we did: lower it one octave. Follow the score as you listen. You may use the accompaniment for your own original fugue if you follow the chord symbols given. It's called *Summerscape Fugue*.

Summerscape Fugue

(Recording No. 33)

BANC

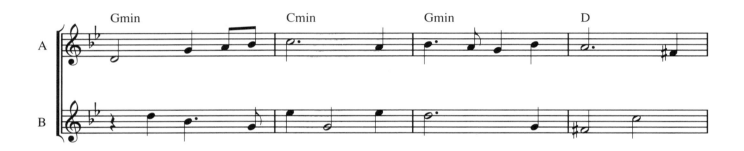

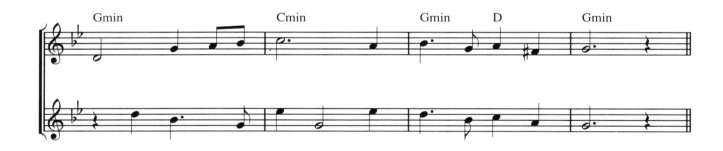

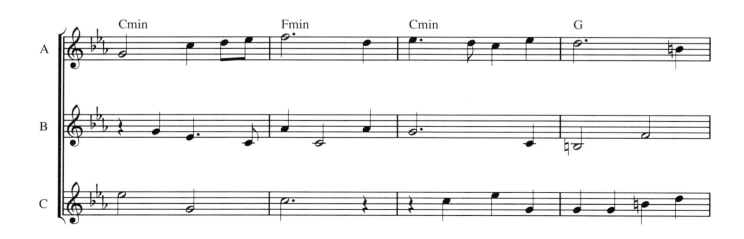

The recording you hear has been done by a string quartet. Any (or at least most) combinations of sounds, will probably work rather well. Finding a dominant theme for a lyrical version will often work well when arranged for mixed voices (S. A. T. B.).

PART V

Writing the Accompaniment: Introducing the Models

Good accompaniments, partner songs, and countermelodies have one thing in common: they supplement the melody and make every effort not to duplicate any more of the melodic line than absolutely necessary.

Generally speaking, it is better to understate than to overstate the accompaniment. The accompaniment is not the main attraction and should subdue itself accordingly. Nuances, subtleties, and inflections often add richer taste to the accompaniment than direct musical statements. In other words, let the melody have its moment—enhance it, beautify it, excite it—but don't stand in its spotlight!

It is generally conceded that the accompaniment and chord structure should be in total agreement, except in use of passing tones, during the course of which there might not be room to include all the chord symbols involved.

Example 1 offers one of the simplest forms of accompaniment writing. Here's the formula: (1) name the chord, (2) use the tonic (root) triad, and (3) root the bass.

Example 1:

(Recording No. 34)

Generally speaking, the bass part is the starting point for any arrangement involving writing an accompaniment. It is the foundation tone on which all else rests.

Traditionally, the most favored bass note is the root, that is, the note involved in the chord's name. The second most favored is the fifth of the chord. The root, for the most part, should be used on the first beat of the new chordal identity.

Write a bass part using the chord symbols as your guide. (Play your bass part along with the recording—it should work quite well!)

Waltz in F

(Recording No. 35)

BANC

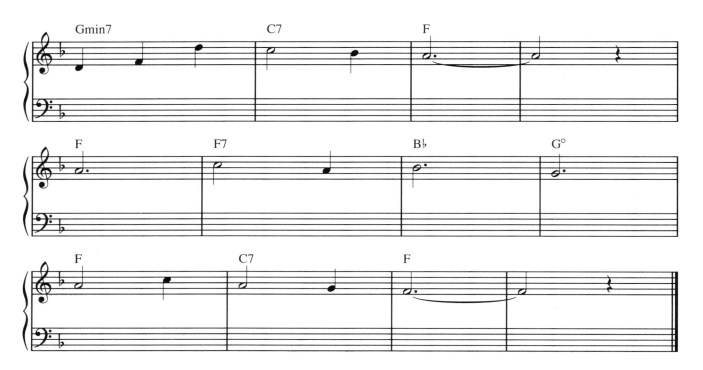

Now that we've established the prime necessity of the bass part in writing an accompaniment, let's see how we might embellish the treble part, too. Let's turn back to example 1 and embellish the chords named.

A slight expansion of example 1 would be to separate the notes of the tonic chord and add the octave note above. Keep the bass root note the same as before (or you might want to lower it an octave at times). This is shown in example 2.

Example 2:

(Recording No. 36)

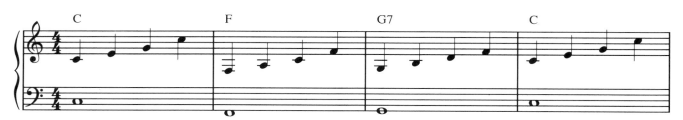

For an even greater change, use the notes of the chord in various orders of sequence; that is, don't follow the root through the chord progression (or 1, 3, 5, 8) but rather mix it up, as you will see happening in example 3.

Example 3:

(Recording No. 37)

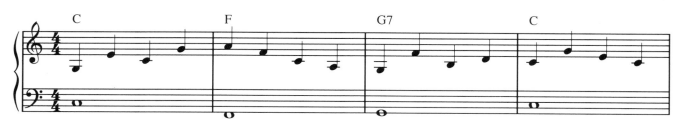

A passing tone is any note that is not normally used in the chord but that acts as a bridge between two notes found in the chord. Passing tones are most effective when used sparingly. Refer to example 4 for good use of passing tones.

The use of passing tones adds an even greater variety of color to your accompaniment. In the following example, it might be assumed that the melody is rather sustained, hence the use of more movement in the accompaniment.

Example 4:

(Recording No. 38)

The accompaniment adds many nuances to the general tone of the song. The following example shows two distinct shades of sound supporting the same melodic line. Both will work, but they create different moods:

(Recording No. 39)

Models: Fitting Your Song in a Form

For those who can compose but who feel a bit unsure about writing a specific type of song, the MODEL is one of the better answers. Here's how it works: A particular type of composition is laid out for you (graphically) measure by measure. All you have to do is fill in these measures with notes that (1) are compatible with the chord structure given, (2) are playable in that particular style (e.g., a conventional hymn would not have a two-octave range), and (3) complete each measure insofar as required beats are concerned.

To whet your appetite, the following pages contain models for a march, a sacred anthem, a standard popular song, a folk song, and a fugue. And, to make your song more exciting, you are assured that your composition is an excellent partner song to the original for which the model has been made. As an example, the march model is modeled after the march *Anchors Aweigh*. The accompaniment to *Anchors Aweigh* will adapt perfectly to your new composition. In fact, a bit further on in this book, you will learn how to transpose. And, in learning this step, you might want to feature your new melody as a countermelody performed by a whole section of the band!

Before you start to write your countermelody to *Anchors Aweigh*, remember a few tips. If the original melody employs half notes, it will sound quite satisfying if you use quarter or eighth notes; and, of course, the converse is true. If, however, your new melody is not intended as a countermelody, write it as you please.

Your fugue model has the number 1 melody carried throughout the four parts. Note that each time this melody line ends its eight-measure sequence, it begins again in the new key suggested by the last note of the above melody line. Remember that the last note becomes the first note of that same melody but that it is now in the new key demanded by the entrance note. The structure of the chord symbols will remain the same; however, the new key will alter its respective names.

When you compose melody number 2, keep in mind that it must conform to the chord structure above melody number 1 in the new key. This automatically harmonizes melody numbers 1 and 2.

Melody number 3 (as well as melody number 4) continues to harmonize with the original melody number 1 (again in new keys following the same chord structure).

The March Model

The accompaniment for this model is played three times so that three separate melodies might be introduced as a playable trio (wait for the little interlude between each of the three parts).

Anchors Aweigh
(Recording No. 40)
(four measure intro.)

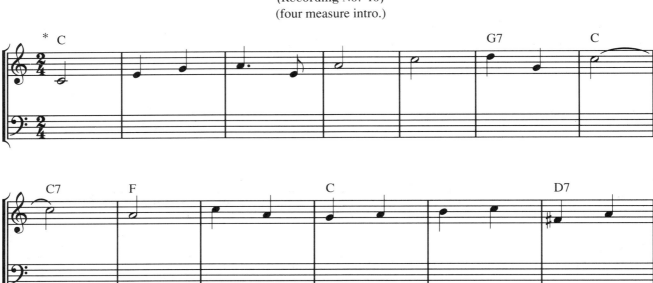

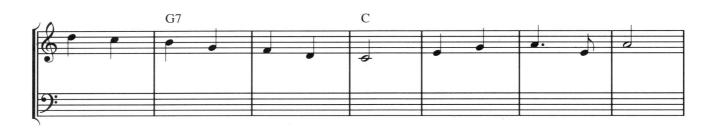

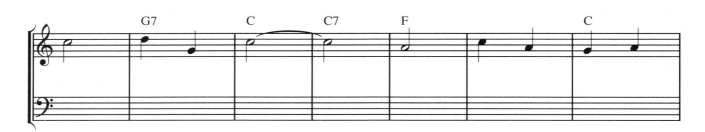

* Continue chord until next change of chord.

The Sacred Model

This model uses the lovely *Lo, How a Rose e'er Blooming* as its format and is arranged SATB for voices. Because they are singing neutral sounds, your composition (following the same chord patterns) will be compatible with it.

Lo, How a Rose E'er Blooming

(Recording No. 41)

Traditional
Lyrics — Praetorius

Model for Standard Popular Song

As with most popular standards, the melody is often played with embellishment. Note the piano playing "lead" (or melody) takes this freedom from the exact, stipulated melody set down. Vocalists also take this freedom more often than not. Arrangers take their freedom, too!

That Wonderful Feeling for Life

(Recording No. 42)

(four measure intro.)

Words & Music by Bob B. Ashton,
ASCAP

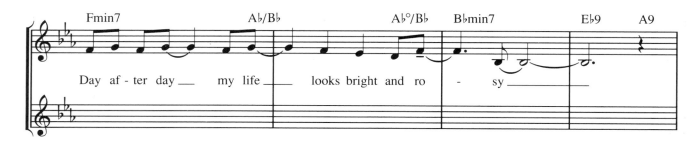

Folk Song Model

There are so many folk songs—and nearly as many styles of writing them —that we singled out one of the best known ones for your model. Have fun with it! (There's a two-measure intro before you begin to sing or write.)

Incidentally, there are two accompaniments. You may choose either the traditional one or the more jazzy treatment.

Someone's in the Kitchen with Dinah

(Recording No. 43)

(four measure intro.)

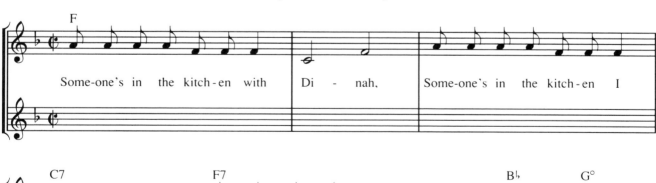

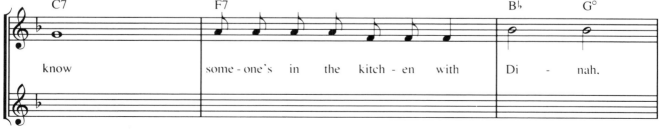

The Fugue Model

(Recording No. 44)

This was recorded using piano and bass as accompaniment. It will work for anything conforming to the chord symbols employed.

Simple Orchestration: Its Component Parts

You will learn most by experiencing the sounds produced from your own writing. Needing a place to start, we should direct you to the simplest approach possible. From the beginning step you will be able to eventually climb the ladder.

Transposition: What Is It?

Basically, transposition is writing music in the proper key for a specific instrument. *Concert key* instruments need not transpose their part as far as key is concerned. Placing these instruments in their proper range is another story. But for now, let's look at some of the more common instruments that play in the concert key, or the key in which the master score is written. Or it may help you if we say the key in which the keyboard instruments play. Here are some concert key instruments:

Piano	Bells
Organ	Glockenspiel
Guitar	Marimba
Violin	Xylophone
Viola	Trombone
Cello	C-melody saxophone
String bass	Oboe
Harmonica	Banjo
Flute	Ukulele
Piccolo	Bassoon

These instruments must be transposed:

Trumpet	All saxophones (except for C-melody)
Cornet	French horn
Clarinet (both B-flat and E-flat)	English horn

The following method will assist in getting your transposition accurately accomplished:

Trumpet	Raise the key signature one full step, then
Cornet	transpose the part the same way.
B-flat clarinet	
B-flat tenor saxophone	

Example (transposing trumpet, cornet, B-flat clarinet, B-flat tenor saxophone)—concert key of F (all will be in the key of G):

Now, for the E-flat alto and E-flat baritone saxophones, you must lower the key signature by three half steps. Example: Concert key of F finds E-flat saxophones in the key of D (count down E, E-flat, D).

Example (transposing E-flat saxophones):

Remember, saxophones cannot play below B—just a half step below middle C—so it often sounds better to transpose to the correct note and then raise it one octave. The previous example for E-flat saxophones would sound very well like this:

Example (transposed and raised one octave):

French horns (whose timbre lies between the trumpets and trombones) can be transposed by lowering the concert key five half steps.

Example: Concert key of C finds the french horns in the key of G (count down B-natural, B-flat, A, A-flat, G):

Trombones usually play in the bass clef, so you will need to write their part as follows:

Note: The trombone part will now sound one octave lower than the treble clef counterpart. To show how the treble clef would be written to duplicate the bass clef sound shown above, the following is shown:

String bass parts can vary greatly according to style. Rooting, plus using the 4th and 5th of the chord, often works well if simplicity is desired. Here's an example of *Mary Had a Little Lamb* done with electric piano and string bass:

Example:

(Recording No. 45)

Now comes the problem of determining what to write for the various instruments. It's really up to you to decide. Virtually any combination will work well if you plan your arrangement carefully. First, let's do a simple exercise to review what we've learned.

Determine the chord for each of the following instruments using concert key as your guide. Remember: when the instrument designated plays any note of the chord named for that measure, it will be completely compatible with that same chord played in concert key. Some of the instruments below will need new key signatures for this to happen.

Compose an original four-measure melody, using the following chord symbols as your guide.

Transpose your original melody for clarinet.

Transpose your original melody for E-flat alto sax.

Transpose your original melody for trombone.

Transpose your original melody for cello.

Starting to Arrange

Now is as good a time as any! It's time you begin an actual arrangement. No, we'll not attempt an entire song as yet—let's just try four measures of an old standard we've used before, *Home on the Range*.

This is not always the case. But, for now, let's follow this procedure: We'll write an arrangement for piano keyboard and then transpose it for trumpet, clarinet, and E-flat alto saxophone.

Because you are only beginning to arrange, it is well to confine your instrumental (and/or vocal) parts as much within the staff as possible. This rule will bend considerably when it applies to keyboard, clarinet, saxophone, and flute.

Let your imagination have some reins! It's not hard to stack the chords, or arrange vertically, as it is often termed. It takes a bit more ingenuity to arrange horizontally.

In examples A, B, C, D, and E, the following structure has taken place:

Example A: This is the lead line (concert key) with chords and words.

Example B: This is a concert key arrangement that has not been transposed for trumpet, clarinet, and alto saxophone. It is strictly an idea put down so you can proof it on the keyboard.

Example C: Here we find a vertical arrangement using a trumpet on the lead with clarinet and alto saxophone on harmony.

Example D: This is the horizontal idea found in example C that has been arranged for keyboard. The horizontal arrangement embellishes the original slightly.

Example E: This is the horizontal idea found in example D transposed.

Note that the original chord symbols have been observed (but structured for the new key). Yes, you could have had either the clarinet or the alto saxophone on the lead and used a different combination for harmony. Experiment with different sounds—it's exciting!

Home On The Range

(Recording No. 46)

(Recording No. 47)

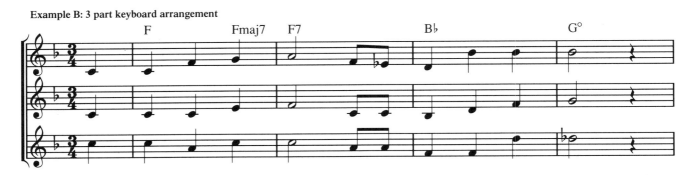

*   Note the use of E-flat rather than E-natural. Some manuscripts use both. Because the chord went to an F_7, we opted for the E-flat version. Later, you'll hear us use the other version in a different arrangement.

(Recording No. 48)

Now, as we begin to embellish the arrangement just a bit, you'll hear some slight dissonance that may (or may not) be compatible with your ear. These dissonant sounds are created by passing tones, that is, tones that are not found in the chord structure, but that are used to find a smooth path to where they intend to go without leaping too far.

(Recording No. 49)

Example D: Keyboard embellished arrangement

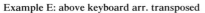

(Recording No. 50)

Example E: above keyboard arr. transposed

*   Most saxophonists don't like any note lower than this "d". In fact, we might have used the "d" one octave higher had we so chosen. Yes, saxophones can be played two steps lower, but they tend to "honk" when played that low. Each instrument has its best playing range, and the careful arranger writes in that better tonal area if at all possible.

Composing and Arranging with the Voice (or Voices) in Mind

Among the most beautiful sounds to be created musically, there are few to surpass those involving the human voice. A broad spectrum of timbre has its potential in this area, and your creativity can produce incomparable rewards. But it takes skill and countless hours of deliberation to consistently achieve the sound you desire.

The following arrangement of *Home on the Range* should demonstrate both how problems come about and how these problems can be reasonably solved. We say "reasonably" because personal taste has so much to do with musical "answers."

Let's first note some chord changes this time around. We've added a new dimension in sound (as far as this song is concerned and its prior use in the text). The second note of the song (above the word "give") has the soprano lead on the note D. This is somewhat low for sopranos (as a lead tone) and their volume might be somewhat weak if they were to sing this by themselves. So we allowed the tenors to sing this one note with them. Granted, it is not really in tenor range either, but with the two parts it will probably sound about right. It should be noticed, too, that all the voices are somewhat at the lower extremity of their easy range. But listen to the lovely sound! Isn't it worth hearing?

The third note of the first full measure has the basses singing an F-sharp. That's not a root note for a G-major 7th chord! But we were looking ahead to the F-natural in the next measure. Our accompaniment was to root the D-flat, so we opted for the F-natural, bringing the bass part right next door to the unison G above the word "where." With this decision in mind, we found the alto part going in a very logical progression from D to D-sharp. This is voice leading in its finest moment, in any arrangement. Why did we go unison after the heavy D-flat 11th? Because the listening ear needs the breathing space.

Now look ahead to the second chord in the third full measure. It has the syllable "fa" to sing. This is the most fundamental position found in choral writing. The soprano and bass are on the same pitch, whereas the tenor sings the third above the alto. This chord cannot miss! It does, however, become boring after too much exposure, and seldom will proper voice-leading allow the transition of parts to fall into place to accommodate this sound. Example: The next syllable "lo" sees the bass and tenor moving to a different position. Why? Look ahead to the word "roam." It was necessary to put our tenors and basses within easy reach of their notes for this chord. Again, no root in the singing bass, so we rooted the chord in the accompaniment! The slanted dotted line signifies that the melody has left the sopranos and has departed for the bass section to carry it.

What do we do if the bass is singing the melody? There are several options, of course, but we chose to close the chord by bringing all the voices in together. Don't worry about the basses having to sing a high D—we've already taken care of that by voice-leading the tenors down to the same note. Between the two of them, it will sound just fine!

Oh, yes, it sometimes is better to have something happening during the course of a long count while holding the same word. So, we decide to add the phrase "where they play"—the final chord change sets up the entrance to the next sequence. Now let's sing through the arrangement and try it on for esthetic size! (Incidentally, in this arrangement we've used the half-step melody line—as we promised earlier in the book!)

Home on the Range

(Recording No. 51)

Traditional
arr. BANC

Some General Hints for Vocal Arranging

(Recording No. 52)

Safe range for bass:

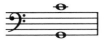

Safe range for tenor:

Safe range for alto:

Safe range for soprano:

Notes above and/or below these ranges can probably be tolerated by most singers, but don't keep them there for long because it's too taxing on the voice.

Generally speaking, the deeper the voice (or wider in timbre), the further the chord spread in use of harmonies. The higher voices (or thinner in timbre) tend to blend well even when voiced tightly together.

Examples: Conventional harmonies

(Recording No. 53)

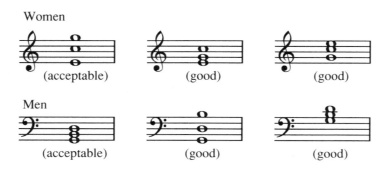

Examples: Dissonant harmonies

(Recording No. 54)

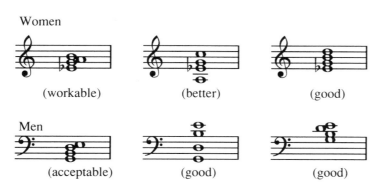

(Recording No. 55)

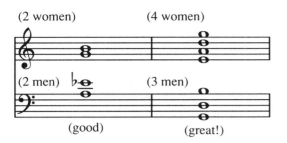

Write an alto part, using the chord symbols as your guide.

All Through the Night

(Recording No. 56)   arr. BANC

Although there are four successive arrangements found in the ensuing pages, the same accompaniment will suffice.

Write a second soprano and alto part, using the chord symbol as your guide.

All Through the Night

(Recording No. 56)

arr. BANC

Write an alto and a baritone part, using the chord symbols as your guide.

All Through the Night

(Recording No. 56)

arr. BANC

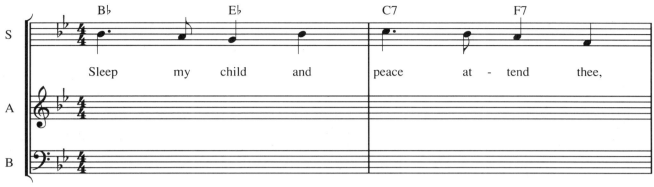

Sleep my child and peace at - tend thee,

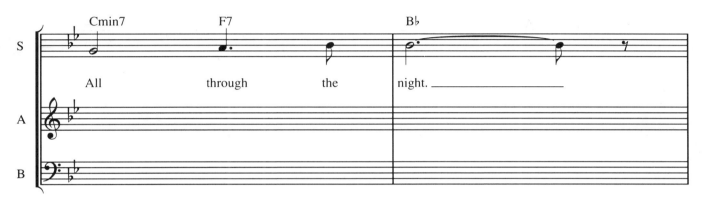

All through the night.

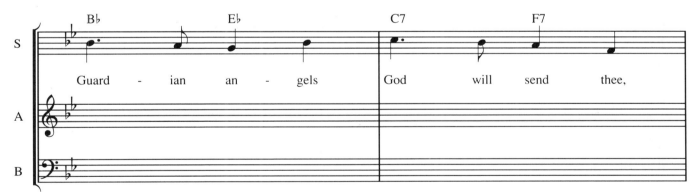

Guard - ian an - gels God will send thee,

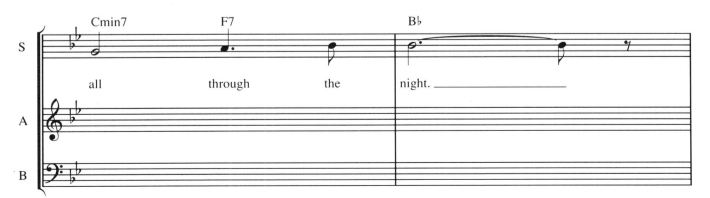

all through the night.

Write an alto, a tenor, and a bass part, using the chord symbols as your guide.

All Through the Night
(Recording No. 56)

arr. BANC

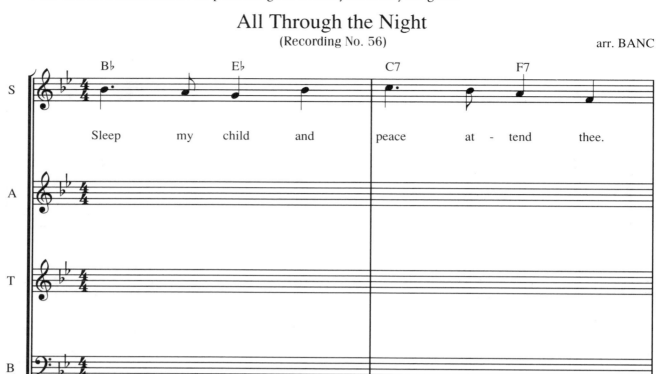

Sleep   my   child   and   peace   at - tend   thee.

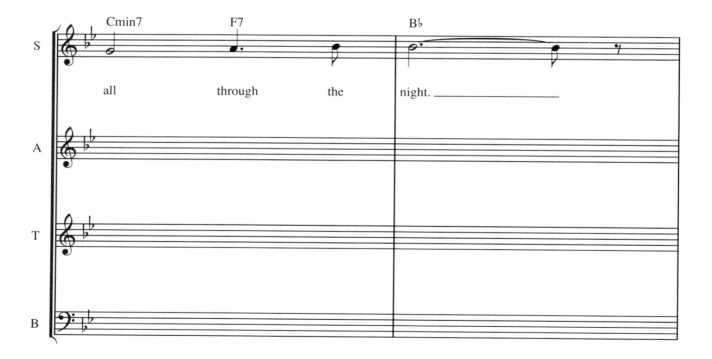

all   through   the   night. _____

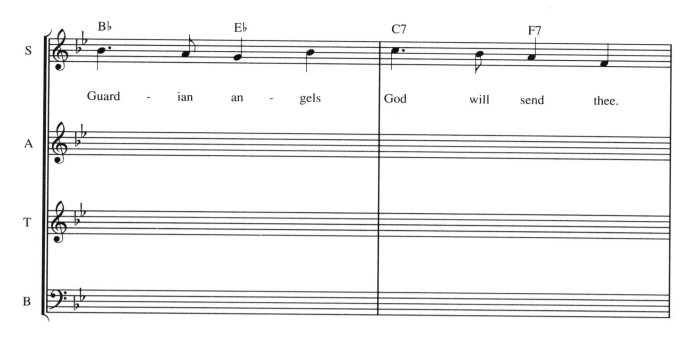

Guard - ian an - gels God will send thee.

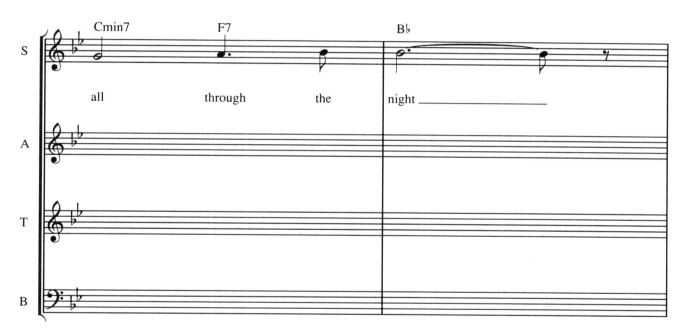

all through the night _____

APPENDIX A

Musicality Test

1. In 4/4 time, a ♩ note gets _____ count(s).

2. In 6/8 time, there are _____ counts to a measure.

3. A dot behind a note increases its value by _____.

4. In 3/4 time, it would require a _____ half note to complete one measure.

5. The name of the fourth line in the 𝄞 clef is _____.

6. The name of the first space in 𝄢 clef is _____.

7. The name of this key signature is _____.

8. The name of this key signature is _____.

9. The name of this chord is _____.

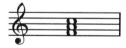

10. The name of this chord is _____.

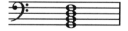

11. In a minor chord, the third of the chord is (raised, lowered) one half step. (circle correct answer)

12. In an augmented chord, the fifth of the chord is (raised, lowered) one half step. (circle correct answer)

13. Name this song:

14. Continue this song as it has been written and used for many years:

APPENDIX B

Chords/Signatures

1. Remember this when naming chords:
   A. Use the bass note as the ROOT (or name) of the chord.

   Example: If you think that F is the note most suited in the bass, use an F chord, that is, F-A-C. Remember: In music, we use only the alphabetical letters A through G and begin all over with A and continue through G, repeating this process over and over. To make up the root chord of any key, simply take your beginning note (root) and skip every other letter of the alphabet (i.e., note), and after three letters, or notes, you have a root triad.

   Example:

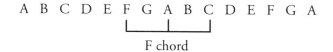

   If you want to use more than a triad (three-part chord), add the seventh letter of the alphabet, counting from the root. If you use a flat with this seventh letter (or step), the chord is simply called a 7th. If you do not flat the 7th, it is called a major 7th.

   Example: An F7 chord would be F-A-C-E♭. An F-major 7 chord would be F-A-C-E.
   B. It is imperative that you observe the key signatures given below. On selecting a root note for your chord name, check the key signature (as in the following examples) and use the appropriate flats or sharps necessary to fulfill the requirements of that key.

   Example: The key of D would have the notes D-F-A. Note: F must be sharped.

2. The following key signatures are for FLAT keys:

   In finding the key signatures for flats, you take the next-to-last flat and call it by that key name (except if there is only one flat, and that key name is F.)

3. The following key signatures are for SHARP keys:

   In finding the key signatures for sharps, you take the note above the last sharp and call it by that key name.

4. The key of C has no sharps or flats. Simply draw a treble clef sign and begin (having placed a time signature).

The following key signatures are for the most commonly used minor keys.

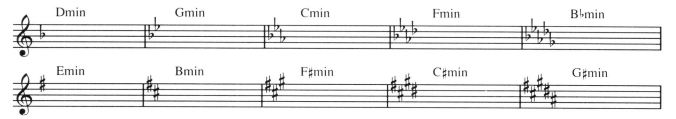

You may have noticed that the same key signatures are used for both major and minor keys, although they are named differently. Each major key has a relative minor, which is three half steps lower and which shares the same key signature.

Example: Key of F (one flat) can also be the key of D minor.

APPENDIX C

Chord Chart

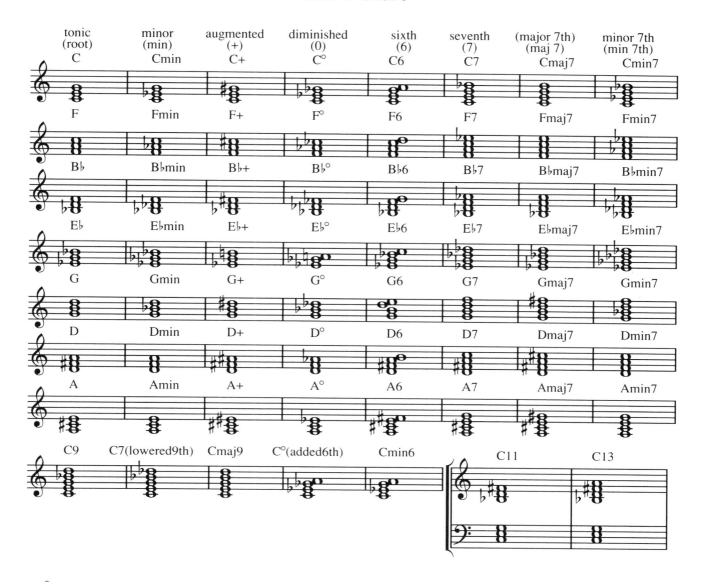

*Other keys follow the above pattern for chord structure. If you can't reach all five notes in the first three chords—C9, C7 (lowered 9th), C major 9—eliminate the bottom note and root the chord in the left hand. In case of chord C11 and C13, it works well to root the triad.

APPENDIX D

Time Signatures

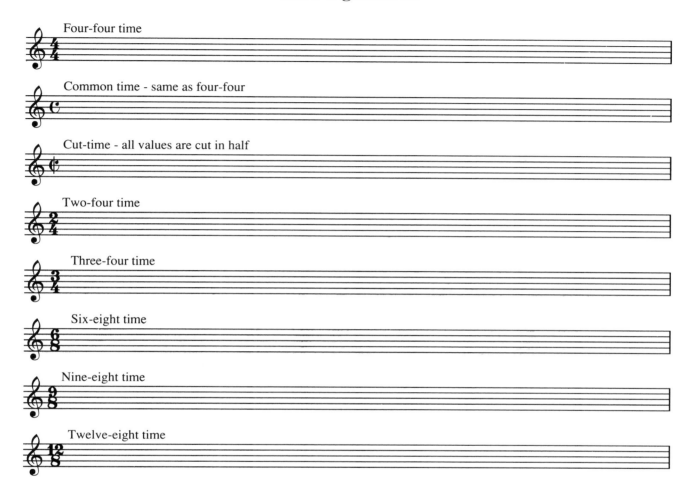

Four-four time

Common time - same as four-four

Cut-time - all values are cut in half

Two-four time

Three-four time

Six-eight time

Nine-eight time

Twelve-eight time

APPENDIX E

Master Arranging Score for Key of C

APPENDIX F

Another Accent Problem

The following excerpt points up the problem of accent. Note the proper accent as conceived by lyric 2 as opposed to the error in lyric 1:

(Recording No. 57)

Apart from the prepositional error ("that" in lyric 1), there is the error of improper accent. The first three notes are musically termed pickup notes and only set the stage for the true opening that occurs on the first beat of the next measure. Here the word "that" receives the accent, and the KEY word "you" comes on the weakest accent of the measure that we have called the pickup measure.

The key word in this song is obviously "you," and it must receive the primary or predominant accent to assure the listener of the writer's intent. Note in lyric 2 that, with only a simple, elementary change, the accent occurs on the key word "you."

APPENDIX G

Answers to Musicality Test (Appendix A)

1. One
2. Six
3. One half
4. Dotted
5. D
6. A
7. G
8. A-flat
9. F
10. G7
11. Lowered
12. Raised
13. Yankee Doodle
14.